# Scramble to Safety

### Alison Hawes ❀ Jon Stuart

## Contents

**OXFORD**

UNIVERSITY PRESS

**Macro Marvel**
(billionaire inventor)

# Welcome to Micro World!

***Macro Marvel*** invented Micro World – a micro-sized theme park where you have to shrink to get in.

A computer called ***CODE*** controls Micro World and all the robots inside – MITEs and BITEs.

A MITE

A BITE

# Disaster strikes!

CODE goes wrong on opening day.
CODE wants to shrink the world.

Macro Marvel is trapped inside the park ...

# Enter Team X!

Four micro agents – *Max, Cat, Ant* and *Tiger* – are sent to rescue Macro Marvel and defeat CODE.

*Mini Marvel* joins Team X.

**Mini Marvel**
(Macro's daughter)

# In the last book ...

- Tiger got thrown into a muddy pool by an elephant!

- He dragged himself out into a tree using his climbing wire.

- The Spider-BITE was in the tree!

**CODE key
(4 collected)**

You are in the Jungle Trail zone.

# Before you read

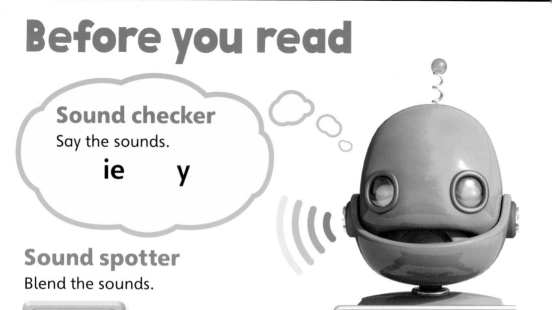

### Sound checker
Say the sounds.

**ie      y**

## Sound spotter
Blend the sounds.

| m | y |
|---|---|

| c | r | ie | d |
|---|---|---|---|

| s | p | i | d | er | s |
|---|---|---|---|---|---|

| t | e | rr | i | f | ie | d |
|---|---|---|---|---|---|---|

### Tricky words
where
who

## Into the zone

What do you think Team X and
Mini will find out about the BITE?

**4**

# The Spider-BITE

Tiger told Mini that the BITE
was a spider.
"I will look it up on my Gizmo,"
said Mini.

# Spider-BITE

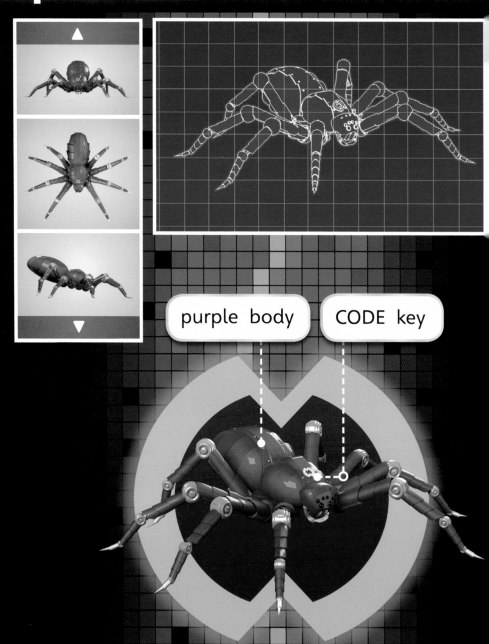

purple body

CODE key

# Where it likes to hide

under piles of rocks

in trees

behind big ferns

# Attack!

Speed · Strength · Combat · Fright

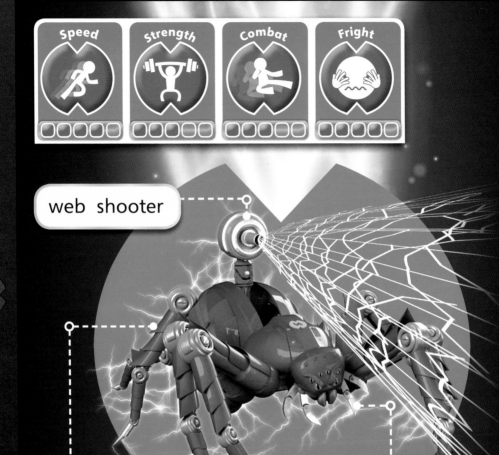

web shooter

raised spikes

This BITE tries to trap its victims in its sticky web.

sharp fangs

It attacks by sending out lots of little Spider-BITEs.

To stop the BITE you have to get the CODE key. Look out!

"We might get bitten by a little Spider-BITE!" cried Tiger. Tiger, who hated spiders, was terrified of this BITE!

Now you have read ...
# The Spider-BITE

## Take a closer look

What have you found out about the Spider-BITE?

What does it look like?

Where does it hide?

How does it attack?

## Thinking time

What do you think is the worst thing about the Spider-BITE? How is it similar to, and different from, real spiders?

Do you think the Spider-BITE is scary?

# Before you read

### Sound checker
Say the sounds.

**ie    y**

## Sound spotter
Blend the sounds.

| b | y |
|---|---|

| s | p | ie | d |
|---|---|----|---|

| r | e | p | l | ie | d |
|---|---|---|---|----|---|

| m | igh | t |
|---|-----|---|

### Tricky words
where
who

## Into the zone

Where might be a good place
to start looking for the BITE?

# Bitten!

Max, Cat, Mini and Rex tried to find the Spider-BITE but it was no longer by the pool.

"Where has it gone?" asked Cat.
"It might be under the rocks,"
replied Mini.

They looked but the BITE was not there.

"Where else might it be?" asked Cat.

"Let's look in the ferns," replied Mini.
"The BITE likes to hide there, too."

Cat spied the BITE by the big ferns. "It has seen us!" cried Cat. "It has released the little Spider-BITEs!"

As they tried to get away, a little spider bit Max on the ankle. "Ouch! My leg!" he cried.

"It says on my Gizmo that we need to rub your bite with this plant," said Mini.

20

"Where is the plant?" asked Max.
"I'll use my magni-beam to find it,"
replied Cat.
Rex flew up to collect some leaves.

Mini rubbed the plant on Max's ankle. It soon healed up.

"Who will look for the Spider-BITE?" asked Mini.

"Not Tiger!" said Cat. "He's terrified of spiders! "Max and Ant, will you go?"

## Now you have read ...
# Bitten!

## Take a closer look

How many words with the /igh/ sound can you find in the story?
Make a table like this:

| ie | y | i | igh | i-e |
|------|-----|--------|-------|-------|
| cried | my | spider | might | likes |

## Thinking time

How did Cat and Mini find the
right leaves to help Max?

Snorp!